Perspectives

Fire
Friend or Foe?

Series Consultant: Linda Hoyt

Flying Start
to Literacy®

Contents

Introduction

How important is fire?

People have been using fire for over 300,000 years: for warmth, for light and to cook food. We also use fire to help us celebrate: we blow out birthday candles, watch fireworks and wave sparklers.

But fire is also dangerous. Bushfires can cause death and injury, and the loss of homes and natural environments.

So, is fire a friend or foe? What do you think?

Fire crackle

Written by Kerrie Shanahan

People have been sitting around campfires for thousands of years, for warmth and because it's relaxing.

Why do we find campfires so relaxing and comforting?

Holly was miserable. She had wanted to sleep over at her friend's house, but her dad said no.

"It's Grandma's birthday," he explained. "The whole family is having a fire and toasting marshmallows!"

"That's so boring!" Holly said and then stormed into her bedroom.

* * * * *

So now, Holly sat grumpily by the firepit. Holly's dad passed her a stick with a marshmallow squished on the end.

"Thanks," she grunted.

Holly watched the marshmallow magically change colour. The fire crackled and danced, and others in her family chatted and laughed. Holly tried to stay grumpy, but she was slowly turning cheerier.

"I'm sorry about before," she said to her dad.

"That's okay, Hol." Her dad smiled. "Now, it's time to get out my guitar!"

Holly pretended to groan, but she couldn't help smiling.

Fire and humans

Written by Joshua Hatch

When our ancestors first learnt how to use fire to cook food, it made a real difference to how they lived. Why do you think fire changed people's lives?

Scientists think our ancestors first discovered fire hundreds of thousands of years ago. They used it to warm themselves.

Ancient firepits suggest people also used fire to cook their food.

Since then, humans have had a special relationship with fire. We use fire for heat, for power, as a weapon and to help make many products. And, of course, we use it to cook our food.

Why was cooking food important?

There are several reasons why cooking was important. One is that it takes a lot of energy for the body to digest raw food. When we digest cooked food, our bodies don't have to work as hard.

Many scientists think the extra energy we get from eating cooked food helped early humans grow bigger brains.

Another benefit of cooking food is that heat kills harmful bacteria. By cooking meat, the food is less likely to make us sick.

Also, cooking food can help it last longer. Cooked food doesn't rot as fast as raw food, so we can save it for later.

Today, we cook food for another reason: cooked food often tastes better. Think about it. Which would you prefer: a raw meat patty or one cooked over a fiery grill?

Speak out!

Fire – friend or foe? Read what these students think.

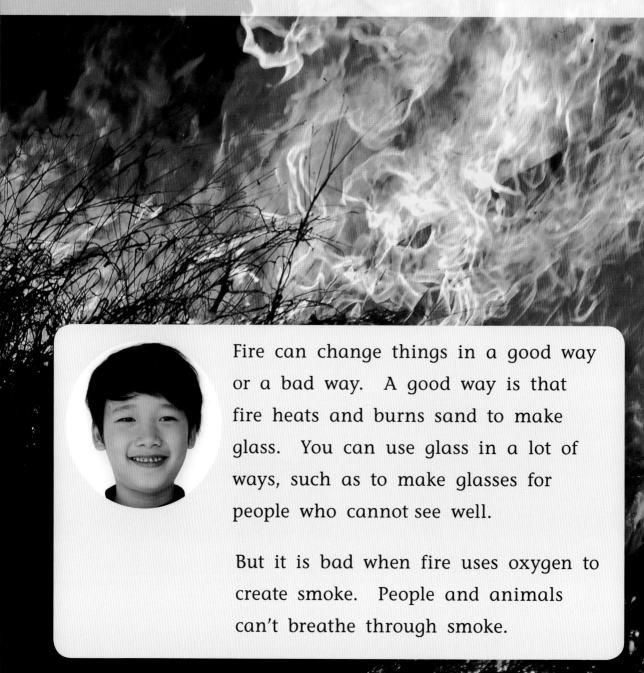

Fire can change things in a good way or a bad way. A good way is that fire heats and burns sand to make glass. You can use glass in a lot of ways, such as to make glasses for people who cannot see well.

But it is bad when fire uses oxygen to create smoke. People and animals can't breathe through smoke.

When fire gets out of control, it can be devastating. Last summer, when it was hot, there were lots of bushfires close to the city where I live. On TV, I saw that many people lost their houses in the fires and it was scary. We could smell the smoke in the city.

When fire is controlled, it can benefit us. It can provide light and warmth. Controlled fire is used in the kitchen, and fire can be used to smelt and shape metal.

Uncontrolled fires can devastate the environment by burning trees and grasses, destroying houses, and killing livestock and sometimes people.

Forest fires

Written by Amanda Shepherd

Fire is nothing to mess with.   Uncontrolled, it can
be dangerous, destructive and scary.   And forest fires
are especially scary.   What could be worse for
trees than fire?

But are forest fires always destructive?   What do
you think?

Forest fires are terrifying to see, but did you know that they are a natural part of forest life? They can even help keep the forest healthy.

Fire clears away underbrush and nourishes the soil. It makes open spaces where young trees can grow and clears the way for sun-loving shrubs that provide food and shelter for many animals.

Fire also helps keep pests in check. Disease and insects kill more trees each year than fire does. A healthy burn destroys those threats.

Though a fire will kill some trees, many survive, because they're protected by thick bark. Most old trees have lived through many fires. Some trees even need the heat of a fire to open their seedpods.

Fire can be a friend to some trees.

How to write about your opinion

State your opinion

Think about the main question in the introduction on page 4 of this book. What is your opinion?

Research

Look for other information that you need to back up your opinion.

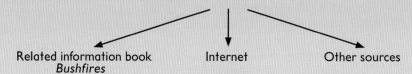

Related information book
Bushfires

Internet

Other sources

Make a plan

Introduction

How will you "hook" the reader to get them interested?

Write a sentence that makes your opinion clear.

List reasons to support your opinion.

Support your reason
with examples.

Support your reason
with examples.

Support your reason
with examples.

Conclusion

Write a sentence that makes your opinion clear. Leave your reader with a strong message.

Publish

Publish your writing.

Include some graphics or visual images.